Optimistic Thinking:

The Key to Success

Rob McCarter

Library of Congress 94–68060

ISBN 1–57087–073–X

Professional Press
Chapel Hill, NC 27515-4371

Manufactured in the United States of America

97 96 95 94   10 9 8 7 6 5 4 3 2 1

Contents

...Many thanks to my wife Selena and to my friends Grayden and Wayne for their invaluable support and advice...also thanks to my sons Jordan and Lawson...you are winners!

Preface

Your mental attitude is one part of yourself over which you have absolute control. By controlling what you think, you can control your success...your life's destiny. "Man alone, of all the creatures on the earth, can change his own pattern. Man alone is the architect of his destiny," wrote Dr. William James.

Many people have the mistaken notion that what they think is merely fleeting notions of little significance. If this is you, then you are wrong! You are the sum of what you think. James Allen, author of *As a Man Thinketh*, said, "A man is what he thinks about all day." Your thoughts result in your attitudes and your attitudes determine your actions. Since we as human beings can control our thoughts, we can ultimately shape our attitudes and ordain our success—or failure.

Entertainer Sammy Davis Jr., titled his autobiography, *Yes I Can!* What a beautiful motto for you to consider adopting. When faced with a challenge that seems to exceed your ability, forget about failure. When you ask yourself, "can I do it?" answer with, "Yes I can!"

Henry Ford once observed, "whether you believe you can do a thing or believe your can't, you are right." What this book is about is developing a positive mental attitude.

Developing a "yes, I can" response to replace negative thoughts. If someone in your life's path says, "It won't work," immediately think of a reason why it will work and a way you will try to make it work.

One word of caution is appropriate at this point. Some positively constructed ideas will not work. This is a fact that an intelligent person has to recognize. However, it is important that you don't discard any idea until you have given it your best. Examine it from all sides. Discuss it with your friends. Prepare a list of arguments both for and against the idea. You may ultimately end up discarding your idea or revising it, but never throw out an idea merely because people subject it to their negative thinking. America is full of individuals who became rich thinking positively about what others thought was impossible or impractical... Their own internal negative thinking led to their lack of success.

In your life you'll make some positive-thinking mistakes—everyone does. But worrying about something after you've done it is the wrong way to adjust your sail in the sea of challenge. If you must, worry first, act and then move on.

A formula developed by Toastmasters International, an organization that cultivates positive attitudes through the practice of public speaking, is a useful one to follow. Their formula is this: Listen, Think, Speak. Stated in another way: collect information; think about the problem; weigh the possibilities; then act. All of these steps are important. But remember, the road to failure in life is paved with indecision. All of the ideas in this book won't do you any good unless you eventually take some action—positive thinking coupled with action!

Surround your goals with a positive attitude. Historian Arnold Toynbee once said, "Apathy can be overcome only by enthusiasm, and enthusiasm can be aroused only by two things: an idea which takes the imagination by storm; and a definite, intelligible plan for carrying that idea into practice."

Next, through the process of positive imaging, focus on what life will be like when you have reached your goal. Create within your mind positive attitudes...positive mental pictures of yourself doing the things you want to do. Experts in psychology all agree that surrounding your goal with positive visualizations causes your subconscious mind to work toward making these mental pictures come true— even while you sleep!

An important psychological principle is at work when you produce a positive mental attitude. Psychologists have discovered that the subconscious cannot tell the difference between an actual experience and a vividly imagined one. Thus, a positive mental attitude begins working to make the actual experience come true in your life.

Another important technique is to act as if you already achieved your goal. Your positive attitude provides a behavior that helps make it happen. If your positive attitude is one of success, then people around you will treat you in the manner of your positive mental projections. These people then become part of your team by triggering important psychological responses inside you which drive you towards your goals.

"It is an important psychological law that we tend to get what we expect," says Dr. Norman Vincent Peale. "If you live expecting bad things, you will get them. This will be true, at least to a degree, because you will mentally, by your expectations, be bringing bad things into being..."

On the other hand, if you paint in your mind positive mental abilities and expectations, you put yourself into a condition conducive to your life's goals. Your mind frees itself from the barriers of negative thoughts and God's might and power are free to work for you.

This book is about developing and using a positive mental attitude. Enjoy!

Wayne Scott, PhD.

Chapter 1

The Beginning

Several years ago I was sitting in a meeting listening to a presentation on dropout prevention which was being sponsored by the school system in which I am employed. At the time, this school system was heavily investing time and money into the prevention of student dropouts. Strangely enough, statistical reports were demonstrating the dropout rate within that system was not different from other systems that were not initiating such lavish programs. The sole exception to the statistical norm occurred in one particular high school. In that school the "dropout" counselor had made significant gains in lowering the dropout rate. Several questions regarding his success ran through my mind as I'm sure they ran through the minds of others in the audience. Questions such as:

Did this counselor work harder than others?

Was he more knowledgeable?

Was he lucky?

Probably the answer to these questions was a combination of yes and no. Attempts to reach conclusions about the role of the counselor's motivation, knowledge, and good fortune in his success led to another important question for me. Was there perhaps an underlying factor or variable that would account for his success?

The active, underlying variable in this case was that the counselor, as a teenager, had been a high-school dropout. He knew from whence the students came. As such he was better able to identify with their thoughts, frustrations, and general boredom with school. He knew that many of these students were jaded to the prospect of a successful future and instead expected a future that was not much better than their current circumstances. It was as if their future was entirely out of their control. Further, he knew that changes would only come in their lives if they changed their expectations from a negative and out-of-control perspective to a positive and in-control perspective. This perspective is called an optimistic thinking style. A style which encourages us to expect the best that life has to offer and to perform the actions necessary to obtain the best. The counselor having had changed his perspective years ago from pessimistic to optimistic was the perfect role model for the students to emulate. It is likely that both in actions and words, he conveyed to them the attitude, "because life is good there are ways to overcome setbacks and more fully enjoy successes."

A Very Valuable Lesson

Thinking back on this counselor's success taught me a very valuable lesson about life and in particular "helping" others. The lesson is this. The most effective motivators of change in other people are those helpers (e.g., counselors, friends, social workers, psychologists, ministers) who once shared a common mindset, albeit a common experience with those whom they are working. They are the role models whose lives tell others who are hurting, "if I can make it so can you."

This realization called into question my ability to help students in my position as a school psychologist in the middle and secondary school level. You see, I have been blessed in life...I have never fought chemical dependency, dropped out of high school or suffered from any other recognized difficulties which can significantly alter a teenager's life.

Personal "Demon"

However, I too fought with my own personal "demon." A "demon" which I believe is the root of most of the difficulties which face everyone. A "demon" that begins in early childhood. One, that if allowed to flourish, will negatively affect us for the rest of our lives. That demon is pessimistic thinking.

In my life, I had learned to expect the worst from every circumstance or event. Little did I realize the effect such thinking was having on me. I didn't realize that by expecting the worst from life I was "inviting" a host of self-defeating actions (e.g., low risk-taking, lack of persistence, compulsive behaviors) and/or feelings (e.g., negative self-image, obsessive thoughts) to accompany me on my life's journey. I was on a downward spiral which would end as an unsuccessful life. A life in which those inner conflicts would result in ineffective living and unhappiness.

Life for me was a vicious cycle of expecting the worse and watching it happen. I believe that, not unlike the global effects of dropping out of school or chemical dependence, pessimistic thinking can also lower quality of life. More specifically I believe that a pessimistic thinking style may be the primary contributing factor in the initial decision to drop out of school or to experiment with chemicals. After all if you expect the worst to happen and it frequently does, then you desperately grasp anything (e.g., chemical use, perceived freedom from school) that may bring about a feeling of control over life. Unfortunately the feeling of control is temporary.

The Evolution

The evolution of my mind, body, and spirit from a primarily pessimistic lifestyle to a primarily optimistic one began, as it does for many, with the caring words of a friend. While in my early twenties a friend said to me, "when you get old you are going to be a grouchy old man." I didn't agree with her but yet her assessment of my character bothered me somewhat. Could she possibly be accurate in her assessment? Was I really a grouchy person? Was I really the type of person that others did not care to be around?

Still not sure of the correctness of her statement, I knew I didn't want to grow old and become a grouchy old man. For I knew that grouchy old men are only grouchy young men who have aged. I didn't realize that what I was experiencing was an extreme case of pessimistic thinking.

However, awareness of a "demon" is one thing. Changing the "demon" is another. I simply didn't know how to make the changes needed in my life. I did what many people in our society do today. I attempted to change the outward expressions (actions, feelings) of my life in hopes of redemption. I quickly learned that changes in outward expressions without a change in thinking is a sure road to failure. Just as the apostle Paul was destined to live with a thorn in his side so was I. Talk about a bright future...

The Revelation

Despite strong pessimistic thoughts, I became relatively successful in college, graduate school, and later in my chosen profession. I had learned to "fake it." I was wearing a mask of optimism.

It wasn't until I began to search for short-term counseling methods to use with high school students that I began to gain insight on techniques that changed my life. My personal transformation began with a review of the work of Dr. Albert Ellis. The crux of Ellis' theory is that our actions and/or feelings happen because of our thoughts and not from the circumstances in our lives. He further states that if we want to change our behaviors and feelings we must change our thought patterns.

Not one to accept any concept at face value, I used myself as a guinea pig to determine if Ellis' theory had relevance and applicability to the real world. It did! My interest and enthusiasm were ignited. I began to read and study everything I could obtain within the field of "thinking psychology."

While Ellis provided the foundation for change in my life, the primary influence came from the work of Dr. Martin E. P. Seligman. Dr. Seligman, a psychology professor at the University of Pennsylvania, initially gained notoriety for his work in the role of learned helplessness as it contributes to depression. A natural evolution of his work led to investigating the role an optimistic thinking style has in deterring depression. Seligman's work resulted in a book called, *Learned Optimism*. Based upon the research findings presented in the book it appears that an optimistic thinking style is perhaps the most important factor in successful people and organizations. People and organizations who expect the best and engage in actions to increase their probability are more successful.

I had found what I had been searching for...methods that would enable me to make permanent changes in the way I viewed the world—a learned optimistic thinking style. I beat the "grouchy old man" syndrome. You can too!

I Can Help, I've Been There

Not only can you beat the "grouchy old man (or woman)" syndrome, but because "I know from whence you came" I can understand and empathize with you. I can help because I've been there. When you have finished this book you will be able to:

- understand the role your thinking style plays in your actions and feelings
- understand that successful living is the ability to solve those inner conflicts which make you ineffective and unhappy
- identify the thoughts which inhibit your life
- identify the thoughts which enhance your life
- learn to question pessimistic and inhibited thoughts
- learn to bolster your life in ways which promote successful and optimistic living

Chapter 2

Epictetus, Epictetus, Wherefore Art Thou Epictetus?

Epictetus was a Greek philosopher in the first century AD who is credited for saying, "Man is disturbed NOT by things but by the views he takes of them." When I first read this, it seemed to make perfect sense. I made a poster of it and put it along with some of the other clever statements and platitudes I had accumulated on the wall of my office. Platitudes such as,

"Expect a Miracle"

"Let us run with perseverance the race set before us."

"Life is what happens to you while you're making other plans."

Not unlike the other platitudes, I had relegated this statement to merely a superficial realm. The realm of positive platitude land. A land of Oz where thoughts, hopes, and dreams exist without actions. Positive platitude land is, in my opinion, a simplistic and shallow view of the world. It's a world in which we give too much credit to the events in our lives as the reasons for our actions and feelings.

Unfortunately I believe this is the level of understanding many people have in their lives today. They live in platitude land and wonder why their lot in life is not better.

It was only after I obtained a clear understanding of the interdependence between life events, thoughts about the events and subsequent actions that I was given a ticket to the train that allowed me to leave platitude land for a more practical and action based plan in life. At this point, I could truly appreciate the intensity and validity of Epictetus' statement. Epictetus had stated in very simplistic yet complex terms the very foundation that was to later become cognitive psychology.

The Thinking Aspect of Man

Cognitive psychology is a theoretical perspective that literally named itself. It is the study of the thinking aspects of man. Very analogous to an atomic bomb, the expanse of knowledge relating to cognitive psychology started from a single point to mushroom into many cognitive areas during the previous twenty to thirty years. The difference in this analogy is that an atomic bomb is destructive while cognitive theory is constructive. Some of the major names in the field of psychology have their roots strongly embedded in its principles. Perhaps all of them owe a debt of gratitude to two people. The first being Epictetus and the second, Dr. Albert Ellis.

It was Albert Ellis who in the mid fifties began to systematically study man from a cognitive perspective, from a thinking perspective. He took Epictetus' belief and modified it to say that a person's actions or feelings are based upon his thoughts.

His pioneering efforts have led to many correlates and postulates which have been and are still applicable to virtually all areas of a person's life. While some improvements have occurred, the essential underlying element is that your feelings and actions are based totally on your perceptions of the event and not on the event per se. Improvements within the field have come primarily in the form of helping people to learn to question inappropriate thoughts and to activate insights into a more appropriate pattern of feelings and actions.

The ABC Approach to Life

An understanding of "how" thoughts affect your actions and feelings must begin with a review of the basic tenets of cognitive psychology. Of particular emphasis will be the work of Dr. Ellis. A working knowledge of Ellis' A-B-C approach to life is essential in order for you, as a reader, to take the next step. The step that ties together how your explanatory thinking style affects your actions and feelings.

As previously mentioned, cognitive psychology is rooted in the thesis that if you are experiencing negative feelings or exhibiting negative behaviors it's because you are thinking irrational thoughts. Thoughts which are based on irrational beliefs (e.g., I must perform well and be loved by significant others; Other people should treat me fairly and kindly; Conditions must be favorable and easy). Ellis' paradigm follows an A-B-C flow of information and is the central focus of his theory of rational emotive therapy.

A=Activating Event

The process begins at point "A". The "A" stands for adversity or activating event. Other names for "A" could include situation, event, or circumstance. We are constantly and consistently bombarded with a multitude of stimuli from outside ourselves. All of the stimuli are competing for our attention. The "A" is in essence anything that is within our environment which we choose to attend. The "A" is always present and as such there will always be a "B" and a "C". No exceptions.

B=Belief

The second component of the ABC sequence is the "B" component. "B" stands for belief. Under Ellis' paradigm, a person's belief is the result of thoughts, ideas, or opinions. Beliefs come in the form of self-talk or self-verbalizations. In other words, beliefs are the result of habitual, repetitive thoughts that we tell ourselves when something happens to us. Essentially, it's what we are thinking when we do not even realize we are thinking.

C=Consequences

The "C" component stands for consequences. Consequences are perhaps the area that offers the most interest to people today because consequences are the outward expressions of our thoughts. For example, we can tell from a person's body language whether they are happy, sad, angry, stressed, et cetera and can reasonably predict whatever action is forthcoming. As such, consequences occur within two categories.

The first category of consequences involves the emotional expressions of our thoughts. Emotions or feelings are considered appropriate when they "fit" the situation whereas feelings are considered inappropriate whenever they are not compatible with the situation.

The second category of consequence involves the behavioral expressions of a person's thoughts. Behaviors are considered appropriate when they "fit" the situation and are considered inappropriate or maladaptive when they do not fit the situation.

A-C Versus A-B-C

Hopefully, you are beginning to understand the interrelationship between the event (A), belief (B), and consequence (C). This understanding is essential because these three components work together to produce either harmony or chaos in our lives.

Chaos occurs whenever we dismiss the importance our beliefs play in our actions and feelings. This interrelationship is called the A-C approach to life and it occurs when we attribute our feelings and actions to the actual event (and not to our belief system). By following the A-C approach, chaos occurs as our actions and feelings sway and change moment by moment as the events in our lives change. A prime example of this type of person is one who is constantly in crisis and appears to never exhibit any control or stability in his or her life.

The second approach to life is the A-B-C approach. This is the sequence that tends to produce harmony in a person's life. Instead of believing we are slaves to the events in our lives, a person who espouses the A-B-C sequence of life believes we can choose how we are going to feel and react to life. In this way the person is in control of his life and can live proactively as opposed to reactively in the A-C style of life.

Why Do People Not Accept?

The question I used to repeatedly ask myself was, "why then, do people not simply accept this and begin to live more harmonious lives?" After much thought and speculation, the conclusion I have reached is that in our society we have been indirectly taught that our feelings and actions stem from the events in our lives. This process is the result of socialization.

Socialization is the methods and means whereby we learn most of our skills at being human. Socialization begins from the moment of birth and is a continuous process throughout our lives. However, it is probably during the first five years of our lives that socialization is strongest for it is during this time we develop our personalities. Our personalities consist of a consistent pattern of characteristics and traits that develop as a result of our thinking styles. Literally, this means the way we explain and interpret the world for the rest of our lives has developed by the time we enter kindergarten.

Our Personalities

What happens during these first five years which significantly influences our personalities? Remember, as infants and toddlers we are totally dependent on others for most of our basic needs (e.g., food, water, safety), for love and nurturing. Those who take care of us naturally become very important to us and we look to them either directly or indirectly to teach us social skills. Direct influence includes thousands of socialization skills. For example we are taught how to eat with utensils, how to talk with others, how to care for our basic needs, how to appropriately make our wants and needs known, how to feel and how to do all these things in a socially appropriate manner. All of these methods are direct and deliberate influences.

While direct influences are extensive, indirect influences are perhaps the more potent of the two in teaching us "the proper way" to perceive the world. The goods, the bads, the rights, the wrongs, the on and on and on are learned in this way. Indirect influences are learned through observing others. We as infants, toddlers and adults watch others and learn from the people in our environment. According to psychologist, Dr. Albert Bandura, if we view someone being successful in a particular action and we feel that we could also be successful performing that action, then we are more likely to attempt to perform that behavior when a similar opportunity arises. One clear example of an indirect influence occurs when a child uses a curse word that he or she has learned from an adult role model. Chances are the child learned this from observing the adult as he or she responded to a particular situation. Children don't always realize a curse word is not a good word, they only know that it must be okay because a significant person in their life used it.

Not only do children learn certain words from others, they also observe ways in which adults interpret situations, all situations—whether the situation is positive or negative. They hear us say things like, "she makes me so mad", or "he makes me so happy", or "that's awful, terrible, catastrophic"

To put it simply, children watch adults. They watch us for the "correct" ways to feel and act. As such they learn how to react and interpret the world from significant others. They learn and come to believe hook, line, and sinker that it is the events in our lives that cause our feelings and behaviors and not what we tell ourselves about the situation. As they are exposed to verbiage that includes absolutes or exaggerations about situations, they will form the beginning of a belief system that gives too much credit to external events in a person's life. A reference base that says feelings and behaviors are caused by outside events and not by our view of them. The connection is only natural because the adults in their lives believe and actively practice this philosophy.

However, all responsibility for children's actions and feelings cannot be blamed on caretakers. For the most part the entire society of mankind acts on this assumption. If in doubt of the veracity of this statement I challenge you to take a walk into the electronic media field of today.

The Message of Our Generation

What messages do you hear? What is the theme of much of the music of any generation? Constant messages appear which tell us that situations or others are responsible for making us feel happy or sad, relaxed or anxious, fulfilled or empty.

The messages are not restricted to the music industry only. They come from television and movies as well. The one-eyed monster is full of programs that are more than happy to tell us that happiness depends on having the right girl, the right guy, this drink, that car, and that if you don't have these things then you will miss out on the happiness they bring. The happiness THEY bring! The point is we are a society of people who have been repeatedly told, trained, and taught that we are dependent on external situations to determine our happiness and contentment with life. When circumstances are not to our liking we are destined to be utterly miserable and can assume that we cannot be happy, content, or fulfilled until circumstances change. Unfortunately many times the situation does not change because the change-agent is immobilized. The change-agent is you.

The Cause of My Misery

I know that despite all of these arguments many of you will still cling to the belief that the events in your life cause you misery or unhappiness. If you do then I beg you to honestly consider the following scenarios:

1) Do you know someone who is in a similar financial, marital or vocational situation who seems to be happier than you? How do you explain this?

2) Do you know someone who is in a worse financial, marital, or vocational situation than you and yet seems to be happy and content? How do you explain this?

Both of these scenarios ask some tough and potent questions. Questions that require honest answers. The world is full of examples of people who are in similar situations or worse than you and yet have the audacity to be happy.

Are they more intelligent than you? No.

Are they more talented? No.

Are they merely too stupid to realize how bad they have it? No.

These are people who are human. They can hurt and be discouraged and disappointed like all of us. The difference is they have discovered, maybe not through books, but from living life that they do not have to be a slave to their "lot in life." They give no credence to the myth that your situation can make you happy or sad. The key for them is not in what happens to them from the external world but what happens between their own ears; their own ability to think and rationalize.

Thinking Is The Key

Thinking is the key. Thoughts or beliefs are the second link in the A-B-C sequence. Tony Robbins in his book, *Awaken the Giant Within* (1991), states that thinking is simply the process of asking questions and obtaining answers. It is my belief this is a crucial and very workable definition. Henceforth, the art of thinking is the question and answer process. Beliefs are formed based upon this process. Thinking is the key component in cognitive psychology, rational emotive training, and in an optimistic thinking lifestyle. It is the component that espouses and exhorts us to learn and understand that our feelings and behaviors are not caused by situations in our lives but how we interpret the situations based on a series of questions and answers.

Characteristics of Irrational Thoughts

It is evident that our thoughts determine our actions and feelings. With this in mind, Ellis asked the question, "Are there specific thought patterns that tend to enhance irrational feelings and actions?"

After much research, Ellis concluded the answer was yes. Ellis found that at the heart of all irrational thoughts was a system of absolutes (e.g., musts, shoulds, have tos, nevers) and exaggerations (e.g., terribles, awfuls, catastrophes). Anytime you find yourself thinking or self-verbalizing in terms of absolutes or exaggerations, chances are your actions or feelings at that particular moment will also be inappropriate or irrational. It is also likely that the intensity, frequency, and duration of the feeling or action will be out of proportion to the actual event.

Life In The Real World

What does all of this talk about the relationship between your thoughts, your actions, and your feelings have to do with life in the real world?

PLENTY!

Rational thinkers live in the real world. They set high standards for themselves and have high expectations from others. Yet they do not set perfection as the acceptable standard. As such they are not immobilized when they or others do not perform perfectly. As Ellis would say they are "perfectly human". This line of thinking allows them to maintain a variety of appropriate behaviors and feelings when bad things happen. They are not immobilized by the situation.

In conclusion, thinking is the most important variable in the situation/thinking/feeling/behaving cycle. Epictetus began the process that eventually led to a revolution that encourages man to make lasting and permanent changes in his feelings and actions. Evidence is abundant to support the contention and the validity of using such a paradigm. A paradigm that has branched off into the area of optimistic thinking.

Thought Provoker

1) Briefly describe a situation in which you reacted negatively only to later find your actions and feelings were inappropriate.
2) What changed about the situation?
3) What does this thought process tell you about the relationship between thoughts, feelings, and actions?
4) What beliefs do you think were predominate in causing your initial reaction?
5) What beliefs do you think were predominate in causing your latter reaction?

Chapter 3

Why Optimistic Thinking?

A person who is an optimistic thinker is one who essentially believes that because life is good there are ways to overcome setbacks and to fully enjoy successes. To make a statement such as this is certainly "nice" but where is the proof that being an optimistic thinker is any more beneficial than being any other type of thinker (e.g., pessimistic thinker)? Does proof exist or is this optimistic thinking stuff just another form of psychobabble?

It is important that one critically examine any psychological concept before adopting its tenets as one's own. The applicability and use of the concept of optimistic thinking should follow the same criteria as any other scientific study. The result of a vast number of research studies to the phenomena of optimistic thinking has led to three primary categories of benefits.

Benefit #1...Achievement/Success

People who are optimistic thinkers have been found to be high achievers. Achievement has been studied in a variety of areas (e.g., college students, insurance sales, professional sports such as baseball and basketball). In each case it has been determined that people who expressed an optimistic thinking style were not defeated psychologically by adversity in their lives. Instead they viewed the adversity as a hurdle to overcome, as merely a temporary roadblock to who they are and where they want to go.

Naturally a view such as this would result in a person being willing to do what it takes to overcome hurdles. These people feel a sense of control over situations. They persevere until they either overcome adversity or at least come to the conclusion they have done everything they possibly could have to alleviate it. In either case they have obtained a sense of satisfaction from giving their best effort.

However, do not be misled and think that optimistic thinking alone will automatically guarantee success. It won't. That kind of thinking is unrealistic and Pollyannaish. A very important second ingredient is needed. This ingredient is inherent talent. Perhaps a discussion on talent will shed some light on this assertion.

Each of us have heard for many years that we can do or be anything we want to do or be. That is pure hogwash. Talent, as defined by Webster, is an ability or a special fitness for an occupation. I suppose you could extend that definition to include any area of interest and not just an area of occupation. Realistically many of us do not have the talent to perform the skills needed to be successful in some areas in which we would like to be. However the degree to which we're able to express our talent will rise proportionately in relation to the level of optimistic thinking skills we have. In other words we can reach our potential in any field of interest if we believe that we can succeed and focus our actions in that direction.

Benefit #2...Health

The relationship between the mind and the body has been a question of professionals from a variety of fields for a number of years. Former Surgeon General, C. Everett Koop, said that over 90% of all health related problems have a cognitive component. In other words many times it's the negative things we dwell on that result in physical problems for our bodies. This is a concept that has been acknowledged by physicians for decades. In a book published in 1954, Dr. John Schindler stated that most of the common symptoms displayed by his patients were due to distress (i.e., pain in back of neck-75%; lump in throat-90%; ulcer-like pain-50%; gall bladder-like pain-50%; gas-99 44/100%; dizziness-80%; headaches-80%; constipation-70%; tiredness-90%).

Distress is perhaps the main by-product of a pessimistic thinking style. The phenomenon of stress dates to prehistoric times when the cavemen were frequently in situations where they either had to prepare to fight the adversity (e.g, saber tooth tiger, fellow caveman) or flee from it. A physiological response was inherent in their bodies which assisted them in whatever action they deemed necessary.

The same physiological response occurs within our bodies today. We are "prewired" to react chemically whenever we encounter a perceived stressor. Thus the body is prepared for action (to either fight or flee). In our society, the need to fight or flee from our stressors are usually not appropriate options. Therefore, instead of actively dissipating the chemical reaction within our body, we internalize it. Internalization, without action, will result in physiological symptoms similar to those Schindler has described. Eventually the body will break down.

How do we gain control of these stressors? We can either choose to empower or disempower the stressor. If we choose to take away the situation's power, then we can effectively stop the chemical reaction that is so dangerous to our physical and mental health. Likewise, our ability to take away the power of the situation depends on our habitual explanatory thinking style...our optimistic thinking skills. Our ability to, when faced with a stressor, think in ways that assure us the stressor is not our fault (especially when it's not), it is temporary, and that it doesn't have to affect other areas of our lives. This interpretation of the events in our lives will disempower the stressor.

Not only will an optimistic thinking style diminish the effects of stress on our lives but a person with an optimistic thinking lifestyle will engage in actions that promote wellness. For example, optimistic thinkers are more likely to exercise, eat the proper foods, and are less likely to drink alcoholic beverages and use tobacco. They are generally aware of the effects of an unhealthy life style and as such diminish the odds of major illness by avoiding the causal agents (e.g., fatty foods, alcohol, tobacco, sedentary lifestyle) of many diseases.

The link between optimism and health is still under study and scrutiny. As recently as two years ago Chris Peterson and Linda Bosio published a book entitled, *Health and Optimism* (1991). In their book they reviewed and conducted studies which explored the relationship between an optimistic thinking style and a person's physical health. One specific study was conducted in the fall of 1984 at Virginia Tech. The study involved 172 undergraduates who were asked to complete an "Attributional Style Questionnaire" (ASQ) and an "Illness Scale." The ASQ and the Illness Scale measured an individual's level of optimistic thinking and number of illnesses in the previous thirty days, respectively. Two follow-ups were conducted. The first was a month later with the readministration of the Illness Scale. The second follow-up was a year later with a letter requesting the number of times the individual had visited a physician for the diagnosis and treatment of illnesses. The results of the study supported the notion that optimistic thinkers are healthier. Peterson and Bosio cited other studies in their book regarding the benefits of optimistic thinking as it relates to the strengthening of the immune system, the fight against cancer, and so on.

One major point of emphasis is that an optimistic thinking style will not prevent all diseases. Even optimistic thinkers get colds, cancer, and other illnesses. What an optimistic thinking style will do is give you an advantage and extra boost in preventing an illness and in fighting its effects once it starts.

Benefit #3...Depression

A person who is an optimistic thinker is less likely to allow the negative events in their lives to result in depression. Depression is so common in our society that it is now called the common cold of mental health. The negative results of depression are broad and can potentially affect anyone. The ability to effectively fight depression is important for several reasons.

The first reason involves the risk of suicide. Not all people who attempt suicide are depressed, but of those who attempt suicide approximately 85% are. Optimistic thinking styles tend to counter this phenomenon. When adversity strikes, optimistic thinkers do not engage in self-talk that leads to permanence, self-blame, and global effects. In other words they do not say things like, "this bad thing is going to last forever, it's awful, I can't stand it, it's all my fault, I'll never be able to live again" which are characteristic comments of one who is suicidal.

The second reason involves the by-products of depression. Depressed people tend to withdraw, function at a minimum, be inner focused, and give up easily. The world is full of examples of men and women who have allowed adversity in their lives to result in depressive symptoms such as immobilization and inactivity.

Why Optimistic Thinking?

Why optimistic thinking? I believe the data on the effects and benefits of an optimistic thinking style speak for themselves. There have literally been hundreds of studies conducted in this area. The majority of these studies support the contention that an optimistic thinking style enhances achievement and health.

Before you misinterpret my point, I'm not saying that research suggests that a high frequency of optimistic thinking is the "answer" to all of human misery and ills for this is not the case. An optimistic thinking lifestyle is not a panacea. You will still have problems and challenges to meet. With optimistic thinking skills you will have the ability to meet and respond to those challenges more effectively. You need to be aware of your own ability to choose whether you will go through life thinking optimistically or pessimistically.

How You Think Is A Choice

The ability to choose brings up a very important point. Your thinking style is a choice. It is not an uncontrollable inherent response. You learn to think as you do! So the ability to be an optimistic thinker in no more a gift from God that being a pessimistic thinker is a curse from Him. Rather it is a learned thinking style. Let me say that again,

Optimism is a Learned Thinking Style!

This news in and of itself is an awesome concept. This means there is hope for everyone. Martin Seligman, in his book, *Learned Optimism,* states this very clearly and succinctly. Literally, if you have acquired a pessimistic thinking style and are unhappy with it, you can learn a new thinking pattern—a pattern of optimistic thinking.

Who needs to be an optimistic thinker? Everyone! Especially those whose lives and/or professions (e.g. sales, management, helping) include a high potential for failure and frustration. Optimistic thinking, in these situations, encourage success through persistence.

Those of us who dwell within the land of optimistic thinking a majority of the time will reap benefits. Even pessimistic thinkers when "suffering" from bouts of optimistic thinking will tend to, at least, temporarily reap some of the benefits. Unfortunately they will tend to view the benefits as temporary or just a stroke of luck, and will, go back into their habitual pessimistic thinking style and lose the long term effects.

Thought Provoker

1) What are some of the characteristics of a successful person?

2) An optimistic thinker is one who operates on a belief system that says, "because life is good, there are ways to overcome setbacks and to more fully enjoy successes." Pick five of those characteristics and explain how this "thinking" philosophy about life enhances the expression of each.

3) Based on this information, how do you think being an optimistic thinker would benefit you?

Chapter 4

What Do We Say To Ourselves?

The message is clear. The beginning of living a more successful life begins with a change in thinking. Lest we misunderstand, a successful life is not necessarily one that is surrounded by an abundance of wealth and material possessions. No, a more accurate measure of a successful life is an individual who has resolved inner conflicts which, in the past, have resulted in ineffectiveness and unhappiness. A successful person is content. If this is the type of successful life you are searching for, then search no more. An optimistic thinking style will promote successful living.

The Million Dollar Question

How do we begin to live a successful life? That's the million dollar question. Yet, the answer is simple. We need to "begin at the beginning."

We began with the knowledge that our thoughts drive our feelings and actions. Knowledge without understanding is useless. Now we must develop an understanding of those thought patterns in our lives which can lend themselves to either pessimistic or optimistic thinking. We will begin the understanding process with a review of the different ways we explain the world.

Way #1
Causal Explanations

What caused this? This is perhaps one of the oldest and most frequently asked questions of all time. Throughout history man has sought to explain life by attributing "cause" or responsibility to his or other's deeds.

The quest for causality continues today. When we hear of a disaster such as an airplane crash or violent murder, we typically and instantaneously ask, "who (what) caused this?"

We, as human beings, have a need to know what causes everything. Causal explanations are those thoughts we use to explain the cause of an event.

The range of causal explanations vary from ME explanations to THEE explanations. ME explanations are those explanations we use when we attribute the cause of an event to either an internal quality (e.g., intelligence, temperament) and/or an external quality (e.g., height, weight, race, socioeconomic status). On the other hand, THEE explanations are those explanations we use when we attribute the cause of an event to something or someone outside of ourselves (fate, luck. etc.).

Way #2
Temporal Explanations

Temporal explanations are those thoughts we use to estimate the length of time an event will affect our lives. The range of temporal explanations vary from "this too shall last" or lasting explanations to "this too shall pass" or temporary explanations. "This too shall last" explanations are given when we see the cause of the event as long lasting or permanent. Conversely "this too shall pass" explanations are given when we explain the event in a temporary way.

Way #3
Extential Explanations

Extential explanations are those thoughts we use to estimate to what extent a specific event will affect other areas of our lives. The range of extential explanations vary from "major difference" explanations to "minor difference" explanations. "Major difference" explanations are those explanations we use when we see the cause of the event as affecting most areas of our lives. In contrast the "minor difference" explanations are given when we see the cause of the event as affecting one or two areas of our lives.

Thoughts...Thoughts...Thoughts

Within these three ways of explaining life events, lie six specific thought patterns that can either inhibit or enhance our lives. These six thought patterns are the ME thoughts, the THEE thoughts, the PASS thoughts, the LAST thoughts, the MAJOR thoughts and the MINOR thoughts.

There are two qualities about these patterns that need clarification before continuing. The first quality refers to the clustering nature of the patterns. Typically, the six thought patterns will cluster into one of two major explanatory styles. The first cluster contains the ME, LAST and MAJOR thought patterns while the second cluster contains the THEE, PASS and MINOR thought patterns. The extent to which our explanatory styles cluster at one extreme or the other will vary proportionately with changes in our actions and feelings.

The second quality lies in the fluctuation of the thought patterns. In essence we have two explanatory styles...one we use to explain problems (e.g., setbacks, troubles) and one we use to explain successes (e.g., triumphs). For instance if we are the type of people who explain most setbacks by relying on the ME, LAST and MAJOR thought patterns we will also likely be the type of people who explain most successes by relying on the THEE, PASS and MINOR thought patterns. This will become clearer as we proceed.

When Problems Occur

THEE Thought Patterns

THEE thinkers are people who explain problematic events in a realistic and objective manner. They do not concern themselves with finding fault or placing blame either on themselves or others. Instead they realize that to place blame for a problem is a waste of time and not conducive to the problem solving process. They also realize that many times problems occur for a variety of reasons; not due to one single factor. The main objective of THEE thinkers is to overcome the problem and move on with their lives.

We can also be THEE thinkers during times of trouble. By learning to limit self-blame or accusatory thoughts, we will be able to approach a problem objectively and with a clear state of mind. We will determine solutions which will either resolve the situation at hand or help us cope with it. In this way, our lives will be enhanced.

Please don't jump to conclusions. I'm not implying we should shirk our responsibilities and refuse to take blame for problems when, in fact, we caused them. Instead, I am saying we shouldn't automatically assume we are the cause of problems we may be experiencing.

Thinking Truism #1: THEE explanatory thought patterns during problematic times will lead to enhanced actions and feelings.

ME Thought Patterns

On the other end of the causal explanation range are the ME thought patterns. When a problem occurs, ME thinkers automatically blame themselves for the problem. They reason the problem wouldn't have occurred if not for personal internal flaws (e.g., lack of intelligence, bad temper) or personal external flaws (e.g., height, weight, race, socioeconomic status, sex).

Unfortunately we find too many people in today's society who exhibit ME thinking patterns. It's as if they are to blame for every problem in their lives or in the lives of those around them. For example, if a child of a ME mother gets in trouble at school, the mother may rationalize it's because she's not a good parent (when she is). If a ME person does not get asked to serve on a committee in their community, he or she incorrectly concludes it was because he or she wasn't smart enough, talented enough, or popular enough and so on.

What do you think the ME style of explaining "circumstances" does to your lifestyle? It devastates you. The primary area of personal devastation occurs in self-image. Our self-image is the mental picture we have of ourselves. It develops as we compare our strengths, weaknesses, competencies, and inadequacies with others.

People who explain problems using ME thoughts have concluded they do not compare favorably with others. Regardless of objective proof to the contrary they maintain these thoughts. As such they exhibit intense feelings of worthlessness, undesirability, and shame. Additionally, if these people attempt new tasks at all they are likely to give up when the going gets tough. The consequences of explaining the world in ME terms can last a lifetime and can lead to feelings of hopelessness and despair.

Thinking Truism #2: ME explanatory thought patterns during problematic times will lead to inhibited actions and feelings.

PASS Thought Patterns

Hope can be defined as an expectation that events in our lives will turn out for the best. Feelings of hope are necessary for successful living. Martin Seligman tells us a hopeless person is more likely to become discouraged and depressed than a hopeful person. In the midst of problems, it is essential we continue to have a sense of hope.

Where does the feeling of hope spring from? Hope originates in our PASS thought patterns. The ability to hope for better days is a by-product of a "this too shall pass" thought pattern. If you want to truly enhance your life, you need to be able to step back, while in the midst of the battle, and realize "this too shall pass". If you are able to do this, you will discover that most of the time trouble does pass and its effect on your life was less than you feared.

Thinking Truism #3: PASS explanatory thought patterns during problematic times will lead to enhanced actions and feelings.

LAST Thought Patterns

While some are "this too shall pass" thinkers, others are, "this too shall last" thinkers. When problems occur for LAST thinkers, they are convinced the afflictions will last forever.

How would you react if you believed you would have to endure a hardship for an indefinite span of time? Chances are you would be immobilized, angry, or depressed. These reactions are typical when we are faced with problems. Yet, while the PASS thinkers quickly overcome these pessimistic thoughts, the LAST thinkers' reactions are long lasting. Within a short time, the LAST thinker begins to explain every problem, whether it is large or small, in such a manner. To determine that problems will last forever destroys a person's hope for change and a better day.

Thinking Truism #4: LAST explanatory thought patterns during problematic times will lead to inhibited actions and feelings.

MINOR Thought Patterns

The optimistic thinking person is one who evaluates the severity of the situation based on objective data. He or she does not quickly evaluate the situation as awful, terrible, or catastrophic. This person is generally able to isolate the problematic situation and deal with it realistically and objectively. For example a MINOR thinker will not allow a problem which occurred at work to negatively affect time spent with his family and vice versa. People whose explanation processes allow them to deal with problems in this way are usually very successful and productive.

Thinking Truism #5: MINOR explanatory thought patterns during problematic times will lead to enhanced actions and feelings.

MAJOR Thought Patterns

There are times when the events in our lives are truly catastrophic and devastating. During these times our feelings of anger, frustration, and depression may be somewhat justified because they are based on objective reality. Feelings and actions based on objective reality, while outwardly may seem to be a sign of a MAJOR thinker, are not. True MAJOR thinkers are those who explain and thus respond to every routine problem as if it were a catastrophe. We meet these people in all walks of life. Every office, church, school, family has at least one such individual.

I am sure you have observed first-hand the effects "awfulizing" can have in a person's life. These are people who tend to judge the most insignificant problems as awful or terrible. They are what I call "molehill to mountain" makers. These people will take the most insignificant conflicts (molehills) and blow them out of proportion to the point where they seem enormous and overpowering (mountains). The consequences of mountain building are pervasive for soon the problem begins to consume everything. They become preoccupied with the particular problem (e.g., worry, guilt, anger, frustration) to the extent that it taints every other area in their lives. Life is not OK for molehill to mountain makers.

Thinking Truism #6: MAJOR explanatory thoughts during problematic times will lead to inhibited actions and feelings."

The Fork In The Road

There is no doubt that troubles, setbacks, and problems can have a devastating effect on our lives. When they occur, we are called to make choices and decisions. These choices and decisions are analogous to a fork in the road in that the direction in which we are traveling ends and we are forced to choose which path will lead us to our destination. A good choice will lead us to successful lives and a wrong choice will lead us to unsuccessful lives. Let's examine two choices we have in reference to explaining problems or troubles.

The Road To An Inhibited Lifestyle

In our study of thought patterns we discovered there are six primary "thinking truisms" regarding the content of thoughts and their relationship to our lifestyles. Of those six, three explanatory thinking styles are pessimistic and will lead to an inhibited lifestyle. To summarize, they are as follows:

Thinking Truism #2: ME explanatory thought patterns during problematic times will lead to inhibited actions and feelings.

Thinking Truism #4: LAST explanatory thought patterns during problematic times will lead to inhibited actions and feelings.

Thinking Truism #6: MAJOR explanatory thoughts during problematic times will lead to inhibited actions and feelings."

If we follow these thought patterns, we are choosing, to explain each and every trouble, problem, trial, tribulation, or setback as being caused by either an internal flaw (e.g., personality deficit, lack of intelligence) or an external flaw (e.g., appearance, color of skin, sex of person). In addition, we are likely to think that unfavorable situations will last forever and will affect most if not all of our lives.

Would this way of explaining problems be conducive to a successful life? I don't think so. Instead of overcoming inner conflicts which make us unhappy and ineffective, this thinking style will result in an inhibited lifestyle. For example we may:

- become a slave to the circumstances in our lives
- expect the worst from life
- be a complainer and whiner
- have a negative self-image
- fail to fulfill our destiny
- be prone to hopelessness and depression
- give up easily

- be easily frustrated
- be obsessive and compulsive
- be a worrier

These are but a few of the consequences of explaining problems in a pessimistic way. I believe you will agree these are not the qualities of a winner. They are not the qualities of a person who lives a successful life.

The Road To A Successful Lifestyle

An inhibited lifestyle does not sound appealing, does it? It's not, especially when we consider the alternative. An alternative involving three explanatory thinking styles which are positive, optimistic and will lead to enhanced thinking patterns. To summarize, they are as follows:

Thinking Truism #1: THEE explanatory thought patterns during problematic times will lead to enhanced actions and feelings.

Thinking Truism #3: PASS explanatory thought patterns during problematic times will lead to enhanced actions and feelings.

Thinking Truism #5: MINOR explanatory thought patterns during problematic times will lead to enhanced actions and feelings.

It's within our power to choose not to focus as much on the cause of the problem as on the solution. Likewise, we can choose to isolate the problem to the situation in which it occurred thus not allowing it to affect other areas of our lives.

Would this way of explaining problems be conducive to a successful life? Certainly! This style of thinking will aid us in overcoming most of those inner conflicts which make us unhappy and ineffective. The ability to explain problems in this way will result in an enhanced and successful lifestyle. For example we will:
- prevent circumstances from overwhelming us
- expect the best from life
- have a positive self-image
- fulfill our destiny
- maintain hope during the rough times
- view problems as challenges
- enjoy life
- have a zest for life
- be persistent
- enjoy accomplishments

Are these the qualities of a winner? Are these the qualities of a person who leads a successful life? Yes!

When Successes Occur

The book of Ecclesiastes says, "to everything there is a season, a time to laugh and a time to cry..." The message the writer of Ecclesiastes is telling us is we will all face problems (crying times) in our lives. However the good news is we will also experience times of happiness and success (laughing times). The way we explain successes in our lives is just as important as the way we explain setbacks. It is through our explanations we are able to either fully enjoy the good life or to desperately wait for the proverbial "other shoe to drop."

The Optimistic Thinker

Optimistic thinkers know how to celebrate! When good times come they are ready for them. They fully enjoy the experience because their explanatory style promotes appropriate self-confidence and self-pride in a job well done. Additionally, their successes are viewed as a sign of successful times ahead. As such they spread the consequences of their success to other areas of their lives.

We can also more fully celebrate life! To do so we need to reverse our thought patterns from the THEE, PASS and MINOR explanatory style (which is appropriate if we are to be successful in overcoming problematic situations) and switch to the ME, LAST and MAJOR explanatory style during times of successes.

Would explaining successes in this way be conducive to a successful life? Certainly! This style of explaining success will allow us to:
- prevent circumstances from overwhelming us
- expect the best from life
- have a positive self-image
- fulfill our destiny
- maintain hope during the rough times
- view problems as challenges
- enjoy life
- have a zest for life
- be persistent
- enjoy accomplishments

I'm sure you've noticed these are the same consequences of the THEE, PASS and MINOR thought patterns. This is "why" we all need two explanatory styles...one for problems and one for successes.

Thinking Truism #7: A ME, LAST and MAJOR explanatory thinking style during times of success will enhance our actions and feelings.

The Pessimistic Thinker

The pessimistic thinker celebrates. Unfortunately not long enough nor loudly enough. Why? Because he does not allow himself to do so. When it's time to celebrate, the pessimistic thinker halts the celebration early because, maybe due to a negative self-image (or false sense of humbleness), he does not take appropriate credit for the success. Additionally, pessimistic thinkers are waiting for "the other shoe to drop" and as such limit the celebration to one or two areas of their lives. For example most of us have wondered what it would be like to win a prize on a television game show. Wouldn't it be terrific? It would be if winners wouldn't immediately worry about having to pay taxes on the winnings. You may find this humorous. However, I have known people who, upon winning something, immediately take this attitude. For them, the celebration has stopped.

Would this way of explaining successes be conducive to a successful life? I don't think so. Instead of fully enjoying and celebrating our successes, we may:

- become a slave to the circumstances in our lives
- expect the worst from life
- be a complainer and whiner
- have a negative self-image
- fail to fulfill our destiny

- be prone to hopelessness and depression
- give up easily
- be easily frustrated
- be obsessive and compulsive
- be a worrier

These are but a few of the consequences of explaining successes in a pessimistic way. The message for us is this. If we are to overcome those inner conflicts which make us unhappy and ineffective, we need to take heed to "thinking truism #8."

Thinking Truism #8: A THEE, PASS and MINOR explanatory thinking style during times of successes will inhibit our actions and feelings.

Explanatory Style=Successful Living

All of us have a personalized and habitual method of explaining the events in our lives. If we are relatively successful in solving those inner conflicts which make us unhappy and ineffective, we are optimistic thinkers. However, if we are constantly involved in an internal state of conflict it is likely we are explaining life in a pessimistic manner. While it may not seem possible, you choose your own fork in the road of life. It's not too late to backtrack and begin to take the fork which leads to an enhanced, positive, and optimistic lifestyle.

Thought Provoker

Activity #1

1) Think back to a time in your recent past when you were faced with a problem or an unexpected setback that occupied your mind with feelings of guilt, despair, worry, hopelessness et cetera.

2) Based upon the information presented above, rate your explanatory style in each of the following thought patterns:

Causal
ME   1   2   3   4   5   6   7   THEE

Temporal
LAST   1   2   3   4   5   6   7   PASS

Extential
MAJOR   1   2   3   4   5   6   7   MINOR

3) Are these ratings reflective of your explanatory style most of the time when you face a problem or setback?

4) Would you like to change your explanatory style when facing a problem or setback?

5) Which thought pattern(s) do you need to work on?

Activity #2

1) Think back to a time in your recent past when you encountered success.

2) Based upon the information presented above, rate your explanatory style in each of the following thought patterns:

Causal

ME   1   2   3   4   5   6   7   THEE

Temporal

LAST   1   2   3   4   5   6   7   PASS

Extential

MAJOR   1   2   3   4   5   6   7   MINOR

2) Are these ratings reflective of your explanatory style most of the time when you experience success?

3) Would you like to change your explanatory style when you experience success?

4) Which thought pattern(s) do you think you need to work on?

Chapter 5
Just the Facts

The first part of this book was written with one major goal in mind. The goal was to emphasize that acquiring a successful and enhanced lifestyle requires the development of an optimistic thinking style. It is only through an optimistic thinking style that we solve inner conflicts which keep us from reaching our potential or from being as successful as we can possibly be.

The catch is we have to choose an optimistic lifestyle. It won't choose us. We must begin to expect the best that life has to offer and then actively go after it. I know for a fact that anyone who sincerely desires to live an optimistic lifestyle can do so. We can make this choice if we are willing to dedicate and practice the precepts of optimistic thinking.

The second part of this book has been written to give you essential tools needed to develop optimistic thinking. Just as a mechanic cannot fix your car without proper tools, you cannot fix your life without proper psychological tools.

The Four Phases To An Optimistic Thinking Style

In order to learn to be more optimistic there are essentially four phases you must go through. To facilitate understanding, these four phases will be compared to the building of a house. I find this to be a perfect analogy. After all, our bodies are, in a sense, our home. The only way to build either house is from the ground up. Once each phase meets the "code" (government standard) the next phase can begin. It can begin only after government inspection. The first phase in the construction process involves laying of the foundation, the second phase involves raising the walls and the roof (i.e., framing), the third phase involves installation of plumbing and the last phase involves wiring for electricity. All four components are essentially interlocked and interdependent on each other. In many parts of the country these are the only four phases in home construction that have to be government inspected. Successful completion of these four phases will enable the addition of some of the amenities. Amenities which include wallpaper, trimwork, plumbing fixtures, paint, and et cetera.

Phase One

The first step in the process of strengthening our level of optimistic thinking and successful living involves laying the foundation. The foundation of a house is without a doubt the most important part of the house. This common knowledge dates back to Biblical times when men were encouraged to build houses upon rock, upon solid ground, and not on sand. Without a firm and solid foundation, the house, regardless of how unique and beautiful, may tilt, crumble, or even fall down. Building a house without a firm foundation will cause structural damage and essentially destroy all other work done on the inside of the home. The foundational qualities of optimistic thinking are much the same. Without a firm internal foundation the gains we make in our external life (i.e., actions/feelings) will be temporary.

The clues for establishing a firm internal foundation can be found in Chapter Two. In Chapter Two we discovered that the way we feel and the way we act is caused by what we think and not necessarily by what happens to us. This is the foundational belief that everyone must realize in order to live happy and successful lives. It gives us, as individuals, responsibility for our actions and feelings. It tells us we have control over our lives.

However, many of us have relinquished our control to events in our lives. We allow events to dictate our lives. We must reclaim control and power. The first vital step in the building process is to reclaim responsibility for our actions and feelings. Reclaiming responsibility essentially means we have found the rock from which to build our lives. We can proceed with confidence in the construction of our total being.

Phase Two

The second phase in increasing our level of optimistic thinking and successful living can be compared to the framing of a house (i.e., raising of walls and a roof). The walls and roof on a house serve a variety of functions. The primary function is to protect the home from environmental elements. The exteriors of homes differ significantly across the world according to environmental needs. For example, in some areas a brick home better protects occupants from environmental elements. In other areas a thatch home may be preferred.

Just as there are different types of exterior structures for homes there are different types of thought patterns. The six specific thought patterns include the ME thoughts, the THEE thoughts, the LAST thoughts, the PAST thoughts, the MAJOR thoughts and the MINOR thoughts. Some thought patterns offer better insulation from the elements during problematic times (THEE, PASS, MINOR) while others offer better insulation during the successful times (ME, LAST, MAJOR). Part of living successfully requires discernment on our parts regarding when to switch from one style to another as the situation commands.

Discernment comes only after we develop an awareness of our thinking style. Awareness which can be developed as we begin to monitor our thoughts, actions, and feelings. An aid in this process was included in the "Thought Provoker" section in the previous chapter. This activity was intended to direct our awareness in identifying thoughts, feelings, and actions associated with pessimistic or optimistic thinking.

However, a more thorough and valid examination of one's explanatory style can be obtained by completing the Attributional Style Questionnaire (ASQ). A copy of the ASQ can be found in Martin Seligman's book, *Learned Optimism*. Only when we become aware of our explanatory styles will we be able to "frame" our lives in the direction of success.

Phase Three

In any house the installation of plumbing is essential. Not only does it bring in water for cleansing our bodies and homes, but it also serves to transport waste out. Within our lives we routinely need to cleanse our bodies of unwanted feelings and behaviors by flushing unwanted pessimistic thoughts down the drain.

The clue to beginning the process of cleansing pessimistic thought patterns can be found in the immortal words of Joe Friday. Joe Friday was a detective in an old television favorite, Dragnet. Friday played the most deadpan and straightforward role I have ever seen. Yet I must admit I thoroughly enjoyed the program. One of my favorite memories from Dragnet was Friday's familiar phrase, "just the facts". This is the essence of phase three.

Looking at "just the facts" is excellent advice not only for detectives but for everyone. The deliberate process of looking at the facts requires us to entail a method that is almost a long lost art for most of us-the method of questioning. I call this method the "Dragnet Technique."

The Dragnet Technique

The "Dragnet Technique" is used to question the validity of our thoughts. One interesting thing about people is they tend to unquestionably accept the validity of their own thoughts as if they were etched in stone. It's as if Moses came down from the mountain with an eleventh commandment which says,

"THOU SHALT BELIEVE EVERYTHING
THOU THINKEST!"

To follow this commandment would be to effectively shut down any possibility of questioning pessimistic beliefs. For example, instead of asking, "How can I make this better?" or "How can I meet this challenge?" we ask, "Why me?" or "What have I done to deserve this?"

The art and benefits of questioning oneself is tremendous. All great leaders and scientists throughout the years became accomplished in their fields due to the persistence of asking questions. Albert Einstein once stated, "the important thing is to not stop questioning."

Questioning is a powerful technique. It is the primary method we use to rid ourselves of waste. It forces us to look at facts and draw objective and alternative conclusions. These conclusions lead to alternative thought patterns which enable new feelings and behaviors to emerge. Pessimistic thoughts are removed from our thinking which result in a cleansing of mind, body, and spirit.

Allow me to say one more time-change will not occur until we ask empowering questions. Empowering questions lead to an honest appraisal of "just the facts."

Just the Facts
Problem Emphasis

Instructions: The next time you are facing a difficult situation, answer the following empowering questions:

Empowering Question Technique #1
"Me to Thee" Theme
Am I the cause of the problem?
____yes ____no

If no, proceed to Empowering Question Technique #2

BUT

If yes, answer the following "just the facts" questions...

a) Why do I think I was the cause of the problem (what internal quality or external quality; or combination)?

b) Where is the proof the problem was caused by me?

c) What else could have caused the problem (alternative)?

d) Why couldn't one of the reasons in "c" be a more valid cause of the problem?

e) Could the problem be a combination of "me" and "thee"?

f) If no, why couldn't it?

Empowering Question Technique #2
"Last to Pass" Theme
How long will I need to deal with this problem?
_____this too shall last   _____this too shall pass

If you checked "pass" proceed to Empowering Question Technique #3

BUT

If you checked "last" answer the following "just the facts" questions...

a) Will this problem last forever?

b) Why does this problem have to last forever?

c) Have I faced a similar problem in the past?

d) Was I successful in overcoming it?

e) If no, why not?
_____severity
_____inappropriate planning
_____other

f) If yes, what factors helped me overcome the problem?

g) Why am I not utilizing these coping factors now?

Empowering Question Technique #3
"Major to Minor" Theme
How much will this problem affect other areas of my life?
_____All of Life (Major)   _____Little of Life (Minor)

If you checked "little of life," to this question and to the other two (i.e., Thee, Pass) your are an enhanced and optimistic thinker in the face of problems...Congratulations!

BUT

If you checked "all of life" then answer the following "just the facts" questions...

a) Why does the problem have to occupy my thinking?

b) Is worrying about the problem helping me solve it?

c) If "yes", explain how worrying helps.

d) Does feeling guilty about the problem help me solve it?

e) If "yes", explain how it helps.

f) How does worrying and feeling guilty about the problem destroy precious moments in other areas of my life?

g) What is a more constructive plan in terms of limiting the problem to the area in which it occurred?

Success Emphasis

Instructions: The next time you experience a successful event in your life...and you want to get the most out of the event...ask yourself the following empowering questions.

Empowering Question Technique #4
"Thee to Me" Theme
Am I the reason for the success?
_____Yes   _____No

If you checked "yes" proceed to Empowering Question Technique #5

BUT

If you checked "no" answer the following "just the facts" questions...

a) Why do I think I am not the reason for the success?

b) What proof do I have the success is due to other's kindness or to luck?

c) Where is the proof the success is not caused by an internal quality (e.g., intelligence, friendliness) of mine?

d) Why couldn't one of the reasons in "c" be a more valid reason for the success?

e) Could the success be a combination of "me" and "thee"?

f) If yes, doesn't this mean I am a contributor to the success?

g) If no, why not?

Empowering Question Technique #5
"Last to Pass" Theme
What length of time did I benefit from the success?
_____long time   _____short time

If you checked "long time" proceed to Empowering Question Technique #6

BUT

If you checked "short time", answer the following "just the facts" questions...

a) Am I still enjoying the benefits of the success?

b) If yes, what are some of the ways I am still benefitting?

c) If no, am I sure there are no ways in which I am still benefitting?

d) If no, why not?

e) Did I use the success as a springboard for more success?
_____yes   _____no

f) If no explain why not.

g) Why do the positive aspects of this event have to end?

h) How can I continue to use the positive aspects of this event to bring about more success?

Empowering Question Technique #6
"Not OK to OK" Theme
How much will this success affect other areas of my life?
_____All of Life   _____Little of Life

If you answered "all of life" then skip this section...

BUT

If you answered "little of life" complete the following "just the facts" questions...

- a) How did this success lead to success in other areas of my life in the past (e.g., motivated, confidence)?

- b) Did worrying about the longevity of the success aid in my enjoyment of it?

- c) Did feeling guilty about the success aid in my enjoyment of it?

- d) How did worrying and feeling guilty about the success destroy precious moments?

- e) What is a more constructive plan for enjoying success in the future?

- f) Who else can I involve in the celebration of my future success?

- g) What other areas of my life can I incorporate future success?

Revelations

Chances are once you start asking questions you will begin to realize that 95% of the time things aren't as awful or terrible as they seem. Another revelation is that events in your life will not always be the way you would like for them to be. When you realize this (and you will), then you effectively rid yourself of many of the unrealistic demands in life (e.g., shoulds, musts, have to's).

That's not to say that you'll go along your merry way and be thankful for the experience of being disappointed, frustrated, et cetera. Wrong! What you will do is get up, dust yourself off, ask empowering questions and either go about your business or try to improve the situation by facing the challenge head on. The point is you will take action and did allow your thoughts to immobilize you.

A Realistic, Rational and Optimistic Outlook

The art of questioning leads to a more realistic, rational, and optimistic outlook on life. It allows you to dispute pessimistic beliefs. Questioning is a technique for now and always. The more you practice it the more it will become a part of your life. It will become automatic. Optimistic thinking will become an automatic explanatory lifestyle. Well, at least automatic on most occasions.

The relationship between questioning and optimistic thinking is evident in the life of everyone who is successful. Successful people are those who have learned to ask empowering questions. Empowering questions enable individuals to meet and effectively handle the minor and major challenges in life.

Conversely, people with pessimistic thinking styles also ask questions. However their questions when facing challenges, lead to answers that can be inhibiting. Prolonged pessimistic answers can immobilize a person and effectively block the showcasing of their talents for all the world to see.

Don't misunderstand me. No one is 100% pessimistic or 100% optimistic. This, I think, is an impossibility. Everyone experiences periods of pessimistic thinking.

Our thinking style is likened to the plumbing in a house. In any house there are times when pipes leak, the water heater wears out, and so on. During these times immediate repairs are needed in order to avoid further damage. Similarly, the same principle applies to people. Many times a "leak" will occur in our life that will, if not "repaired", eventually result in damage to our body, soul, and mind. Remember, just as there are four phases in the building of a house, there are four phases in the building of an optimisitic thinking style. The third phase, the phase of asking empowering questions and receiving empowering answers, will result in temporary gains without the final construction phase which is the phase of activation. Lest we not forget, optimistic thinking is the tendency to expect the best based on actions. Expectations are primarily the focus of phase three. Phase four brings action.

Chapter 6

Doing: The Final Phase

The final phase in the building of a house involves installation of electricity. Once electrical wiring is in place the builder has progressed to the point where sheetrock can be hung and light fixtures and receptacles can be installed. The house is ready for a permanent power source. The issuance of power signals the end of the construction process and the beginning of the transformation of a house into a home.

The structure is sound and strong. The successful completion was made possible by the experienced builder who understands the importance and interdependence of each phase.

The interdependence that exists is analogous to the relationship that exists between questioning and the fourth phase, the activation phase. Synonyms for the word activation are "activate" or "active". To be active is essentially what phase four is about.

Phase four calls for us to jumpstart or activate our optimistic thinking to successful lifestyles. Lifestyles which will give us more power or control over our lives than we could ever imagine.

In order to activate our lives, we must begin by asking ourselves empowering questions. Questions that spur answers and change. To begin the final phase, simply ask yourself, **"What must I do to activate my life?"**

There are three basic activation areas that, if taken into consideration, will result in an increased level of optimistic thinking and an optimistic lifestyle. These three areas have been put in the form of questions. They are:

1) "What needs to be done to resolve the challenge?"
2) "If I can't resolve the challenge, what can I do?"
3) "What can I do to strengthen my overall level of optimistic thinking?"

The answers to each of these questions are not mutually exclusive. By this I mean that a solution to one of the questions may also be a solution for another question. Be flexible in your strategy choices. Use what works for you. Additionally, the strategies presented are not exhaustive. There are others. These are merely the ones I have found to be effective. Feel free to delete and add strategies as needed.

Activation Question #1
What Needs To Be Done To Resolve The Challenge?

If there is one truism in life it is that everyone has problems. The poor have problems, the rich have problems, the religious have problems, the atheists have problems, movie stars have problems, construction workers have problems...there are no exceptions. Everyone's problems are different. Yet the common denominator in all situations is that problems stem from an individual's interpretation of the problem and not the problem itself.

If we explain problems pessimistically we will become overwhelmed and immobilized. On the other hand, if we explain problems optimistically we can turn problems into challenges and solve, or at the very least, manage them. This alternative leads to activation.

One of the activation techniques I have learned from my readings is the importance of semantic exchanges. A semantic exchange occurs when we take a potentially immobilizing word (e.g., worry) and change it to another more empowering word (e.g., concern). For example to say, "I am worried about Bill" is more immobilizing than to say, "I am concerned about Bill." The word "concern" denotes an implied call to action; the word "worry" does not.

Let's apply semantics to problems. I would like for you to exchange the word "challenge" for problem." I realize from a surface aspect the changes appear to be insignificant. Let me assure you they are not. A semantic change in words from "worry" and "problem" to "concern" and "challenge" respectively does not diminish the severity of the situation(s). However this small change does enhance a person's thoughts to a more workable mindset. This semantic exchange empowers a person to say, "what needs to be done to resolve this challenge?" Thus a person's creativity is not limited as the challenge is met.

There have been many systematic strategies developed to assist individuals and groups in the process of facing challenges. The one strategy I have found to be the simplest and most effective is espoused by Robert Schuller. In his book, *Tough Times Never Last, But Tough People Do!* (1983), he details a technique called the "possibility thinking game." Schuller's reference to the activity as a game is a good example of semantic exchange. The word, "game" is often associated with fun just as the word, "possibility", for most of us is associated with adventure and exploration. Thus a game which involves adventure will spur creativity and solutions quicker than a problem solving activity would.

The Possibility Game

I have taken the possibility game and modified it slightly to make it more amenable to a search for, "just the facts". As such it is in question form.

The Possibility Thinking Game
Question Edition
1) What challenge am I currently facing?
    (be as specific and objective as possible)

2) What strategies can I use to meet this challenge? (brainstorm and list ten ways in which the challenge can be met)

3) Of the ten, which would work best for me? (choose the one that would produce the highest probability of success)

4) What next?
    (implement your strategy)

5) Did it work?
    (if no,...either modify the strategy, choose another strategy, or manage the challenge)

The Possibility Thinking Game will work...but only if you work. The results are almost magical. The game, when played within a group of people, will pay off in a shared vision of success. The impossible will look truly possible and enthusiasm will be at an all-time high.

Activation Question #2
If I Can't Resolve The Challenge
What Can I Do?

The process of solving challenges is an exciting and rewarding pursuit. Yet, there are times we can't resolve the challenges presented to us. There are too many factors beyond our control.

I imagine the phrase, "out of our control" may sting just a bit. Whether we admit it or not most of us want to exert control over our environment. This is OK when we're focusing on ourselves. In these situations it is advantageous to our mind, body, and spirit to have control over our thoughts, feelings, and actions. This is a good thing and it contributes to an optimistic lifestyle.

However, if we're dependent on controlling other people or on waiting for things to be the way we want them to be before we can be happy, then we are out of luck. This criteria of happiness will end in perpetual sadness, frustration, et cetera. This is because people seldom, if ever, allow others to control them. In general, situations we cannot control far outweigh situations we can control. People tend to view uncontrollable people and situations as "problems."

What do you do with people or situations you cannot control?

You simply MANAGE!

The word manage when used as a verb means "to direct." Synonyms include to conduct, to regulate, to guide, to supervise, and interestingly enough, TO CONTROL. Could it be that when we manage a situation we are in essence in control of the situation? Yes. The difference is we are controlling our own thoughts and not the circumstances. As such we are not allowing ourselves to be caught up in false expectations that others in the world have to be a certain way before we can be happy, satisfied, successful, and so on. I think Tony Robbins said it best in his book, *Awaken the Giant Within* (1991), when he stated that one of the difficulties with man is that he has too many rules for negative feelings and not enough rules for positive ones. We need more rules to give us an excuse to be happy and less rules to make us sad.

One of the ways we can begin to follow Robbins' advice is to learn to manage uncontrollable people and situations by managing our thoughts. The main method of doing this is through diversion techniques. Have you ever been so engrossed in something that you lost track of time and essentially blocked out everything else in your life? If so, you have been exposed to a diversion technique. Many people become engrossed with the television. However, others may persue more constructive pursuits such as hobbies, volunteering, sports activities et cetera. The point is this: If you can block out unwanted thoughts during these times, why can't you block out unwanted thoughts in other more difficult times?

I conclude that you can if you choose to! I realize many times this is easier said than done...yet it can be done. The next time you're facing a situation that seems to be out of your control, try a diversion action technique.

Diversion Action Technique

1) Describe a problem you are facing that you cannot solve.

2) Have you exhausted the possible solutions generated from the "possibility thinking game"?

3) Does it help to dwell on the problem?

4) If yes, how will it help solve the problem?

5) If no, then involve yourself in an action that:
   a) is totally unrelated to the perceived disturbing event
   b) is something you have done in the past.
   c) is something that requires total concentration and involvement
   d) is something that involves your total being

Activation Question #3
What Can I Do To Strengthen My Overall Level Of Optimistic Thinking?

As stated, everyone faces challenges each and every day. Fortunately, most of these challenges do not require us to stop in the middle of the situation, (or immediately after), and engage in the possibility thinking game or in the diversion action technique. We are able through automatic questioning, fact finding, and activation to swiftly overcome whatever challenge is presented to us and move on.

We can only do this as we seek to strengthen our overall level of optimistic thinking. This process is facilitated through a variety of activation techniques that serve primarily as preventative measures. The preventative measures strengthen our overall level of optimistic thinking; thus buffering us against unexpected challenges. Let's examine these activation techniques, or what I refer to as "positive reinforcers," in Chapter 7.

Chapter 7

Positive Reinforcers

Activation Technique #1
Contribute

Skeptics can say what they choose about Biblical teachings, but I find they contain a wealth of wisdom. Perhaps one of the strongest principles contained within the Bible is that of the importance of making a contribution. To contribute means to give of your time, talent, and money to others. The times when I have felt the most optimistic and positive about myself is when I have given of myself to help others.

The hope of society rests in our willingness to contribute. The words of a television clown come to mind, "all we have in this world is each other." I challenge you to CONTRIB-UTE. If you truly want to increase your quality of life give to others. Give of your time, talent, and lastly your money. Yes, I mean money is to be the last thing you contribute. If you give of your time and talent, I believe that monetary needs of organizations will automatically take care of themselves.

Additionally, teach your children to give to others. Their level of optimistic thinking and positive self-esteem will increase as a result. There are many programs in your community that you and your children (if you have them) can become involved in. My sister has been involved with her children for several years in delivering meals to elderly shut-ins. Her enthusiasm and dedication has inspired my two sons and me to become involved. My boys love it and want to deliver meals everyday instead of once a week. They are diligent and enthusiastic in their duties. Their lives have been positively affected and will continue to be positively affected in ways I will never know. Giving to others increases our feelings of self-worth.

CONTRIBUTE NOW!

Activation Activity #1

1) What percentage of your time, talents, or resources do you give to others?

2) Are you satisfied with your contribution?

3) Describe a time when you have contributed to others. How did this make you feel?

4) How can contributing to others increase your level of optimistic thinking?

5) How can contributing to others enhance successful living?

Activation Technique #2
Read

While in college I lived, under the assumption that upon graduation, I would have learned everything I ever needed to know about psychology. I could sit back, relax, and enjoy the fruits of my labor. It wasn't long after when I discovered I was wrong. The more knowledge I acquired, the more I realized how little I knew. This is true even now. Everytime I read a book I gain a different perspective on an aspect of human behavior. This is very exciting. So exciting in fact that it's difficult for me to go in a bookstore to browse. I always find a book that I just "have" to read. I believe one of the crucial aspects of strengthening a person's level of optimistic thinking has, at its very core, the thirst for knowledge. Knowledge that is acquired partially through the writings of others and partially through experience.. I have found that reading is truly fundamental. It opens up new worlds, new ways of thinking, new looks at old ways of thinking, and genuinely is an essential skill needed for survival in this world. My hat goes off to those who open up the world of reading to the illiterate population. They are ultimate contributors.

A list of recommended readings which have meant a lot to me in the inspirational and self-help areas can be found at the end of this book. You may also find them helpful.

Activation Activity #2

1) Do you have a "thirst for knowledge"?

2) If no, why not?

3) If yes, how do you satisfy it?

4) How can having a "thirst for knowledge" increase your level of optimistic thinking?

5) How can having a "thirst for knowledge" enhance successful living?

Activation Technique #3
Develop a Sense of Humor

It has been said the only characteristic that separates man from other animals is his ability to laugh. There is a lot of truth and wisdom in this statement. Man's ability to laugh has been related to a variety of physical and mental health benefits. According to Psychologist Laurence J. Peter, "there are two effective ways to get immediate relief from emotional stress. One is laughter and the other is deep relaxation" (*The Laughter Prescription*, 1982). Peter further states that laughter is beneficial to man in ways such as:

- keeping aches and pains from intensifying because it takes a person's attention away from the pain
- stimulating the cardiovascular system
- reducing muscle tension
- promoting healing
- stimulating the brain to produce endorphins, a neurotransmitter, that act as a natural opiate in the body

While laughter is truly beneficial, the ability to see humor in situations is possibly more important because your sense of humor originates from your thinking style. It's virtually impossible to develop a sense of humor if you explain life pessimistically.

Knowing this, Peter developed a prescription for developing a sense of humor. I have slightly revised his prescription and have included it as an activation activity because it essentially represents what I have found to be personally useful in strengthening and maintaining an optimistic lifestyle.

Activation Activity #3

1) Do you have an attitude of playfulness?

Adopt an attitude of playfulness. This does not mean you will do outrageous things but that your mind is open to uncensored, nonconformist, silly or outrageous thoughts.

2) Do you think funny?

Think funny. See the funny side or flip side of every situation. Select and refine your outrageous thoughts that best expose your conceits, sense of self-importance and differences.

3) Do you laugh at the incongruities of life?

- Laugh at the incongruities in situations involving yourself and others.
- Only laugh with others at what they do rather than for who they are, unless you are assured they can laugh at themselves for who they are.
- Laugh at yourself, not in ridicule, but with objectivity and acceptance of self.

4) Do you take yourself too seriously?

Take yourself lightly. Take your job and your responsibility to yourself and others seriously. You will discover this will make life's anxieties and burdens lighter.

5) Do you make others laugh?

Make others laugh. By creating happiness for others, you will experience a special joy of accomplishment that only a lively, generous sense of humor can bring.

6) How can the expression of a sense of humor increase your level of optimistic thinking?

7) How can the expression of a sense of humor enhance successful living?

Peter concludes his prescription by exhorting us to realize a sense of humor is deeper than laughter and more satisfactory than comedy. It delivers greater rewards than merely being entertaining. A sense of humor sees the fun in everyday experiences. It is more important to have fun than it is to be funny.

I believe that Laurence Peter has discovered what many other people in life have discovered. Nothing in the world equals the attractiveness and charisma of a person who has a sense of humor. A person who can evoke laughter and humor into everyday life will brighten the day for those around him. Additionally, these people tend to focus on positives, they see things optimistically.

Activation Technique #4
Take Care Of The Spirit

There are essentially three parts to man; the mind, the body, and the spirit. Unfortunately, in our modern Western society man is more concerned with the mind and the body than he is with the spirit. This is a mistake. Without a spiritual basis, I do not believe that man can truly live an optimistic lifestyle. Spirituality, in itself, is based on a positive expectancy and a work ethic. In essence, it is intricately tied to the concept of optimistic thinking. There is no stronger source of positive expectancy than the assurance of a greater and more powerful being. One on which we can rely in times of extreme challenge. Man's quest for spirituality will aid him in developing wisdom and character. Anthony Robbins (1991) states a person's life values serve as a personal compass for his behavior. Just as a compass is used in life to direct our path and to help us when we are lost, so are our values used to guide our decisions.

Anyone who is truly admired and revered is one who allows his spiritual values to help accentuate his optimistic lifestyle. When I think of all the people who have positively influenced my life, I think of those who are not only optimistic but who also stand for something. People who live by the golden rule.

A prime example is a man named Archie. Archie is a successful businessman who has owned and operated an automobile body shop for many years. He once told me he started the body shop in a garage in his back yard. He built his business by offering his customers quality and service. Within a few years, his business had grown to the point in which the back yard garage was too small to accommodate his customer's needs. He expanded the business by relocating to a larger facility. Archie is a success. He is a success in his personal and professional life.

What is the secret of his success?

The answer is simple. Archie is an optimistic thinker who did not abandon his spiritual values for a quick buck. He knew that service and quality are extensions of the spiritual precept of, "do unto others as you would have them do unto you." He also knew that providing this type of service to others would lead to success.

The world is full of "Archies." People who build their character and wisdom upon spiritual values. It is my wish that every single person has had at least one "Archie" to emulate in their lifetime. If you have, you have been blessed. If you haven't, you need to find one. Maybe you are an "Archie" yourself. Maybe you can serve as a role model for someone else. This status is earned and not given to you. Use your earned status and contribute. The world appreciates you whether you realize it or not.

Activation Activity #4

1) Do you know an "Archie"?

2) What qualities does your "Archie" (he or she) possess that you'd like to acquire?

3) How can "taking care of the spirit" increase your level of optimistic thinking?

4) How can "taking care of the spirit" enhance successful living?

Activation Technique #5
Learn To Imagine

As a child can you remember lying in the grass and staring up at clouds?

Do you remember all the different shapes that came into view as the clouds moved across the sky?

What has happened to you since then?

Do you still watch clouds or are you too busy?

Do you still imagine?

Chances are it's been years since you've relaxed in this way and let your imagination run wild.

Guess what! The clouds are still there....and so is your imagination. Your ability to imagine didn't go away, it's just lying dormant and waiting for you to awaken it.

In today's world the purposeful attempt to imagine is called "imaging." Imaging is a technique that essentially requires a person to progressively relax his body and to imagine.

Imaging techniques come in one of two methods. They can be either undirected or directed. Undirected imaging is similar to the cloud watching memory. A person begins by progressively relaxing the muscles in his body. Once relaxation is accomplished the person allows his imagination to run free. In this way one does not try to block thoughts. Instead, he welcomes them and allows them to come and go at will.

The second imaging method is more directed. This happens when, after relaxation, our thoughts are focused in a particular area. The late Dr. Norman Vincent Peale called this, "positive imaging." He stated, "it consists of vividly picturing in your conscious mind a desired goal or objective and holding that image until it sinks into your unconscious mind, where it releases great untapped energies." (*Positive Imaging*, 1982).

Imaging works. The difficulty most people experience in the process of imaging is due in great part to their lack of knowledge of the "how to's" of imagining. There are many effective resources available that teach the techniques of imaging. Most of them work. Personally, I have found the audible cassette tapes to be extremely effective. Robert Griswold, President of Effective Learning Systems, has developed a series of tapes which focus on the imaging aspect of your life (e.g., visualization power, weight loss, goal setting, stress management). On each tape Griswold takes one through the stages of progressive relaxation and then offers suggestions geared to a particular area of concern. These tapes can be very beneficial.

Discover the value of imaging. Discover the need to spend time each day in the quietness of yourself. This will truly enhance the quality of your optimistic lifestyle. It works, try it.

Activation Technique Activity #5

1) Have you ever been lost in your thoughts?

2) If yes, how long has it been?

3) Have you ever deliberately engaged in "positive imaging"?

4) If yes, what were the advantages of positive imagining?

5) If no, try it for daily for one month.

6) How can learning to imagine increase your level of optimistic thinking?

7) How can learning to imagine enhance successful living?

In Conclusion

In conclusion, the purpose of chapters 6 and 7 was to present activation techniques that would answer three basic questions:

What needs to be done to resolve this challenge?

If I can't resolve the challenge, what can I do?

What can I do to strengthen my overall level of optimistic thinking?

I challenge you to pick anyone whom you admire (an Archie) and ask him or her each of the following questions:

1) How do you meet and solve challenges presented to you in your life?

2) How have you handled challenges you felt were beyond your control?

3) How did you develop your optimistic outlook on life?

4) How did you solve inner conflicts which made you unhappy and ineffective?

I guarantee you the person you talk with will give you answers similar to the strategies presented in this chapter. In all likelihood, if you're lucky, your "Archie" will share even more creative ideas with you.

Chapter 8

You CAN!

The ability to live a successful life is not merely a pipe dream but a real possibility. Throughout this book we have defined success as the measure of one's ability to resolve those inner conflicts which make one ineffective and unhappy.

Many of us go through life measuring success in terms of prosperity, fame or wealth. While these are nice amenities to add to our lives they do not determine our true success. If they did there would not be unhappiness or dysfunction within affluent circles.

The irony is it's possible to have it all...both peace of mind and prosperity. We can have it all and fully enjoy our successes. It all begins at the thinking level. In this book we have been repeatedly reminded that optimistic thinking is the key to success. IT IS!

Lest we forget there are nine major points which will aid you in becoming an optimistic thinker.

Point #1   Our actions originate as a result of our explanatory style (thoughts).

Point #2   Our feelings originate as a result of our explanatory style (thoughts).

Point #3   Our explanatory style is learned.

Point #4   An optimistic explanatory style will allow us to solve those inner conflicts which make us unhappy and ineffective.

Point #5   Those who have solved those inner conflicts that have made them unhappy and ineffective are those who lead successful lives.

Point #6   If we are unhappy and ineffective we, too, can learn to explain life in a different way.

Point #7   Thinking can be defined as asking questions and obtaining answers.

Point #8   The first step in changing thoughts is to become aware of the pessimistic explanations we give and to actively question their validity.

Point #9   The second step in changing thoughts is action. Changing thoughts without action, is temporary.

My Hope

It is my hope this book will point out the validity and importance of optimistic thinking. Bear in mind, an optimistic thinking style does not guarantee a challenge free life. We all face challenges. During these times we must "dig in" and persevere.

My hope for you is that you have read this book with interest and with a renewed spirit and dedication to enjoy all that life has to offer...to live a successful life. I'd like to leave you with a selection written by Charles Swindoll.

Attitudes

The longer I live, the more I realize the impact of attitude on life.

Attitude, to me, is more important that facts.

It is more important than education, than money, than circumstances, than failures, than successes, than what other people think, say, or do.

It is more important than appearance, giftedness, or skill.

It will make or break a company...a church...a home.

The remarkable thing is we have a choice every day regarding the attitude we will embrace for that day.

We cannot change the past...we cannot change the inevitable.

The only thing we can do is play on the one string we have, and that is our attitude...

I am convinced that life is 10% what happens to me and 90% how I react to it.

And so it is with you...we are in charge of our ATTITUDES.

References

Anthony, Robert. *Doing What You Love, Loving What You Do.* Berkeley Book. New York. 1991

The Bible.

Dyer, Wayne. *Your Erroneous Zones.* Avon Books. New York. 1977

Ellis, Albert, Y Becker, Irving. *A Guide to Personal Happiness.* Wilshire Book Company. North Hollywood, Calfornia. 1982.

Glasser, W. *Taking Effective Control of Your Life.* Harper and Row. New York. 1984

Kranzler, Gerald. *You Can Change How You Feel.* RETC Press. Oregon. 1974.

Kushner, H. *When All You've Ever Wanted Isn't Enough.* Pocket Books. New York. 1986.

Peale, N.V. *Positive Imaging.* Fawcett Crest. New York. 1982.

Peter, L.J. & Dana, B. *The Laughter Prescription.* Ballantine Books. New York. 1982.

Peterson, C. & Bosio, L. *Health and Optimism....* The Free Press. 1991.

Robbins, A. *Awaken the Giant Within.* Fireside Books-Simon and Schuster. New York. 1991

Schuller, R. *The Be-Happy Attitudes.* Bantam Books. New York. 1987.

Schuller, R. *Tough Times Never Last But Tough People Do.* Bantam Books. New York. 1983

Schuller, R. *Success Is Never Ending Failure is Never Final.* Bantam Books. New York. 1988.

Schwartz, D. *The Magic of Thinking Big.* Fireside Edition. New York. 1987

Seligman, M.E.P. *Learned Optimism.* Knopf Publisher, New York. 1990.

About Rob McCarter

Rob McCarter helps people learn essential life skills while simultaneously challenging them to maximize their potential. Rob's desire to make a difference in people's lives led him to specialize in psychology. With a master's degree in psychology, he has worked for over twelve years within the public school system as a school psychologist. In addition, he spent ten years as an adjunct psychology instructor at Limestone College. He is currently serving as an adjunct psychology instructor at Gaston College.

Through his work with people of all ages, Rob discovered the principles he espouses in his workshops which he offers through his consulting business, Life Enhancements. Principles centering around the development of an optimistic thinking style as a prerequisite to success. According to Rob, "success cannot be measured in the material trappings of this world but in the degree to which people are able to solve those inner conflicts which make them ineffective and unhappy." Rob teaches methods which allow participants to reduce those inner conflicts which block success. He believes it is essential for people to develop the philosophy, "because life is good there are ways to overcome setbacks and to more fully enjoy success."

Rob is a parent, author, coach, teacher, husband and wonderful storyteller. An expert in the field of optimistic thinking and the role it plays in success, Rob would be happy to talk with you about the needs of your organization and to offer services which would assist you. If you are interested in scheduling Rob for a workshop or speaking engagement you can contact him at:

Life Enhancements
PO Box 363
Belmont, NC 28012
704-825-4400